THE RUBBER BAND BALL

THE RUBBER BAND BALL

FINDING **FREEDOM** THROUGH THE ATONEMENT OF JESUS CHRIST

RON HOWARD

For information and comments, contact the author at:
therubberbandballbook@gmail.com

Printed by
Y Mountain Press

Visit the website for a free PDF download of this book,
and to listen to the audio recording:
therubberbandball.com

Cover design by Ron Howard
Interior book design by Francine Platt, Eden Graphics, Inc.

Paperback ISBN (color) 978-1-611662-58-0
Paperback ISBN (black & white) 979-8-89454-129-7

Library of Congress Number: 2026909089

Manufactured in the United States of America

First Edition

DEDICATION

To every son and daughter of God who has
carried more than they were ever asked to carry.

To those who thought strength meant silence.

To those who believed pain meant punishment.

To those who quietly endured.

And to my eternal companion—
whose steady devotion, gentle faith, and
quiet strength have reminded me
again and again who I am.

Author's Note

If you had known me as a boy, you would not have predicted I would write a book.

English was my hardest subject. I had more energy than attention. Today it might be called ADHD, but back then, it was just "Ron has the attention span of a gnat."

My favorite subjects were lunch and recess.

So when the prompting first came to write this book, I dismissed it.

Then it came again.

And again.

I'm not a professional writer.

I'm a storyteller.

And I have spent years watching what happens when people stop carrying what they were never meant to carry.

I have watched shame lift.

I have watched anger dissolve.

I have watched faces that were once heavy become light again.

This book exists because I have seen what the Atonement of Jesus Christ actually does—not in theory, but in living rooms and bishops' offices and quiet moments of surrender.

If you are carrying something, I want you to be healed.

As you read this book, have a spiral notebook to list what I refer to as your "rubber bands." Then you'll begin to learn the process of removing them.

CHAPTER 1

No One Sets Out to Build a Rubber Band Ball

It doesn't begin with rebellion.

It doesn't begin with open defiance.

It begins with something much quieter.

It begins with influence.

In the Garden of Eden, before Adam and Eve "hid" their nakedness from God, there was no temptation.

The serpent approached Eve with suggestion, distortion, and half-truth.

He did not force.

He enticed.

He questioned what God had said. "Yea, hath God said . . . ?"

That is how temptation works.

It introduces doubt.

It reframes the truth.

It minimizes consequence.

Sometimes temptation comes through thoughts.

Sometimes through environments and sometimes through other people.

Not all rubber bands form because we wake up wanting to sin.

Sometimes they form because someone persuaded us, pressured us, manipulated us, mistreated us, or acted unrighteously toward us.

Satan tempts. People misuse agency. And we find ourselves in situations we never intended.

After Adam and Eve partook of the fruit, the scripture records,

And the eyes of them both were opened, and they knew that they were naked; and they sewed fig leaves together, and made themselves aprons" (Genesis 3:7).

Notice the sequence:

Temptation.

Choice.

Consequence.

Hiding.

They felt exposed.

Vulnerable.

Ashamed.

And instead of immediately turning toward God, they attempted to manage it themselves.

They sewed fig leaves.

That was the first self-made covering.

The first "I'll handle this."

The first rubber band.

But here's something important: Not every rubber band comes from your own sin.

Some come from what others did to you.

Eve was tempted.

Adam chose.

Both felt exposed.

Sometimes you were tempted.

Sometimes you were persuaded.

Sometimes you were wounded.

Sometimes something was done to you that you didn't choose.

Rubber bands form in all of those situations.

Because whether we sinned or were sinned against, the next step is often the same:

We cover.

We hide.

We internalize.

We carry.

We replay.

We say,

"I should have known better."

"I should have stopped it."

"I can't tell anyone."

"I'll just deal with this myself."

And the rubber band ball begins.

Satan's work doesn't end with temptation.

If he can't trap you in the act, he'll trap you in shame.

If he can't destroy you in the moment, he'll attempt to bind you to the memory.

That is how rubber bands multiply.

Christ came to break those bands in both situations.

He didn't come only for the sinner.

He came for the wounded.

Alma 7:11 teaches, He took upon Him:

"Pains and afflictions and temptations of every kind."

Temptations.

Pains.

Afflictions.

Whether you were enticed, or hurt, or ashamed, or regretful—

The pattern afterward is the same:

We try to manage it alone.

And that is where the rubber band forms.

One becomes two.

Two becomes ten.

Ten becomes a ball.

The more rubber bands we try to hide.

The bigger the ball gets.

The bigger the ball, the more it affects us.

And it affects everyone around us.

Where Mine Began

My rubber band ball began when I was a young husband with more determination than wisdom.

We were expecting a baby girl.

There were bills to pay.

School unfinished.

I would wake up at four in the morning and go move sprinkler pipes in potato fields.

If you've never walked through wet soil before sunrise, let me describe it. The ground clings to your boots.

The metal pipe feels colder than the air. Your hands ache before the day even begins.

Then I would take my pregnant wife to her mother's house and drop her off. Later, she would walk half a mile to the preschool, where she would earn a dollar an hour for the next eight hours.

Then I'd go to school at ISU.

Then the cheese factory, where the smell would settle into your clothes and follow you home no matter how many times you washed them.

Then to the gas station to pump gas.

Then maintenance work at the Roadside Inn.

And on weekends, I played in a band.

I wasn't bitter.

I was hungry.

Hungry to provide.

Hungry to succeed.

Hungry to prove that I could build something meaningful.

One day, while working maintenance, I helped a gentleman carry boxes into a hotel meeting room.

He was selling World Book encyclopedias.

I asked him if he made any money doing that.

He pulled out his W-2, showing $123,000.

This was the early 1970s.

Gas was 25 cents a gallon.

For that same quarter, you could get a movie ticket, soda, and popcorn.

That number hit me in the chest.

"That's a real job," I thought.

When I told my mother I was going to sell encyclopedias door to door, she said kindly:

"Well, maybe someday you'll get a real job."

She didn't mean to wound me.

But it landed.

And inside me, something wrapped.

"I'll show you."

That sentence fueled me for years.

It built a drive.

It built ambition.

But it also built something else.

A rubber band tied around identity.

Christ once said:

"Come unto me, all ye that labour and are heavy laden, and I will give you rest" (Matthew 11:28).

Notice the order.

Come first.

Rest second.

Pride reverses that.

Prove first.

Rest later.

That is how the ball begins.

Accountability

It's important to understand something clearly

Acknowledging temptation does not remove accountability.

Influence is real—but agency is still ours.

Satan entices.

Others may cause pressure.

Circumstances may be unfair.

But we still choose.

Sometimes we've chosen poorly.

Sometimes we've stayed silent when we should have spoken.

Sometimes we've walked further than we intended.

And sometimes we were simply wounded by someone else's choices.

The purpose of recognizing influence is not to shift blame.

It's to understand how the rubber band formed.

Because until you understand how it formed, you will not know how to release it.

Christ does not excuse sin.

He redeems it.

He does not minimize pain.

He heals it.

Both require honesty.

CHAPTER 2

Do You Know Who You Are?

Not long after I was promoted to division manager, something happened that shaped me more than any sales training ever could.

The western zone manager—a senior vice president over thousands of division managers—was coming to work with me for a day.

Out of all the managers across the western United States, he chose me.

I was young.

Ambitious.

And, if I'm being honest, proud of being chosen.

We were scheduled to meet at a small restaurant in Pocatello, Idaho.

When I walked in, he was already seated at the counter, speaking with a gentleman next to him. I didn't want to interrupt, so I quietly sat on the other side and listened.

The man beside him worked at a steel mill. He was describing his job in detail.

He supervised thirty men.

He carried responsibility.

He made $25,000 a year.

In that era, that was respectable money.

He wasn't just sharing information—he was declaring importance.

Then he asked the zone manager a question.

"What do you do?"

I remember thinking, Oh no. You just asked the wrong question.

Because the man sitting beside me wasn't just a salesman; he oversaw the entire western region.

He earned far more than $250,000.

He carried influence and authority most people would never see.

I braced myself for a subtle but decisive response.

Instead, he smiled and said simply:

"I sell World Book encyclopedias."

The steelworker blinked.

"Can you make any money at that?"

The zone manager nodded gently.

"I've done very well. It's been good to me and provided a good life."

That was it.

No title.

No hierarchy.

No comparison.

Just calm confidence.

The man said he needed to get back to work—"Those thirty guys aren't going to manage themselves"—and left.

Once the man was gone, I turned immediately and said, "Why didn't you tell him who you are? You're over this whole western United States! You probably make ten times what he makes. Why didn't you tell him that?"

He looked at me steadily and said something I've never forgotten.

"I know who I am. I don't need to prove that to anyone."

Then he paused.

"Do you know who you are?"

It felt like someone had pressed a finger directly into my chest.

Because if I were being honest, I didn't fully know.

I was still trying to prove it.

I was proving it to my mother.

Proving it to former teachers, neighbors, even myself.

Every promotion felt like validation.

Every ranking felt like an identity.

Every contest win felt like oxygen.

And every setback felt like suffocation.

That's a dangerous way to live.

Because when your identity rises and falls with performance, peace becomes temporary.

Romans 8:16 teaches:

"The Spirit itself beareth witness with our spirit, that we are the children of God."

That identity doesn't fluctuate with numbers.

It doesn't collapse with a bad quarter.

It doesn't inflate with applause.

It's covenant-based.

But at that stage in my life, I was still performance-based.

And the rubber band ball was getting bigger.

CHAPTER 3

ZERO

THAT VERY WEEK, the zone manager and I visited three areas where we launched one of the biggest sales contests of the year—the last-year-model sale.

It was a major push.

Kickoff meetings in Boise.

Pocatello.

Idaho Falls.

Energy was high.

He stood beside me as I cast vision. I felt confident. Supported. Ready.

Then the first day's numbers came in.

Utah—under a good friend of mine—had already sold 100 sets.

Idaho?

Zero.

The second day's report arrived.

Utah—climbing fast.

Idaho?

Zero.

Numbers themselves are neutral.

But interpretation is not.

I had an appointment that afternoon in Rigby, Idaho, with a schoolteacher to train him on how to sell World Book encyclopedias.

But instead of driving straight there, I took a detour and pulled into a Walmart parking lot in Idaho Falls.

I sat in the car.

And I cried.

Not because of the numbers.

but because of what I told myself about them.

"What kind of leader am I?"

"I'm the youngest division manager in the company."

"The zone manager just stood beside me."

"And we've sold nothing."

Discouragement doesn't shout.

It whispers.

"Maybe you're not cut out for this."

"Maybe you were promoted too soon."

"Maybe you've hit your ceiling."

I seriously considered driving home.

No one would have known.

But *I* would've known.

Galatians 6:9 says:

"Let us not be weary in well doing: for in due season we shall reap, if we faint not."

If we faint not.

That's the decision.

Discouragement feels like a feeling.

But it becomes powerful only when it becomes a decision.

I wiped my eyes.

Started the engine.

And drove toward Rigby.

I took the back roads and drove really slow.

On the way, I saw a house with toys in the yard.

Years earlier, someone had told me:

"Toys mean kids. Kids mean education."

I almost drove past it. But then I pulled over.

Knocked on the door.

When the woman answered, I said half-heartedly,

"I'm selling World Book encyclopedias. I don't suppose you'd be interested . . ."

I had already started to turn away and leave.

"Wait," she said. "I do want some."

Her daughter had recently become sick and would be home for a month.

"How soon can I get them?" she asked.

I stepped inside.

Gave the presentation.

Sold a full set.

I drove down the road and stopped at another house—a woman running a small hair salon in her basement.

Sold her, and also the woman getting her hair done.

Three sets in less than an hour.

Momentum shifted.

But more importantly, perspective shifted.

I got on the phone.

"They've been buying like crazy in Utah," I told my team. "Well guess what? They just started buying here today. I've sold three in an hour! If you're going to get to the potential customers before someone else does, you better get moving."

By the end of the contest, our division finished number one in the entire company.

Number one.

And I still shudder at how close I came to quitting in that parking lot.

One decision separated surrender from surrendering.

One rubber band of discouragement almost redirected my whole life.

CHAPTER 4

Comparison is a Rubber Band

When Utah reported a hundred sales and Idaho reported zero, the problem wasn't the numbers. The problem was comparison.

Comparison is one of the fastest ways to build a rubber band ball.

It feels harmless at first.

It even feels motivating.

But it quietly wraps identity around someone else's results.

When I sat in that Walmart parking lot, I wasn't just looking at a report.

I was measuring myself against another division manager.

And in my mind, I was losing.

Comparison distorts perspective.

As James 3:16 teaches,

"For where envying and strife is, there is confusion and every evil work."

Comparison creates confusion.

Confusion creates insecurity.

Insecurity tightens rubber bands.

When you compare, you begin interpreting:

"They're ahead. I'm behind."

"They're better. I'm less."

"They're succeeding. I'm failing."

But heaven doesn't measure you against your neighbor.

When Samuel went to anoint a king, he looked at Eliab and assumed he was the right choice.

But the Lord corrected him:

"For the Lord seeth not as man seeth; for man looketh on the outward appearance, but the Lord looketh on the heart" (1 Samuel 16:7).

God measures faithfulness.

We measure performance.

That difference alone builds entire rubber band balls.

Comparison also has another side.

Sometimes it fuels pride.

"I'll show them."

"I'll outrun them."

"I'll beat them."

That can produce results.

But it cannot produce peace.

When your identity depends on outperforming someone else, you will always be unstable.

Because someone will always be ahead of you in something.

True identity is anchored in covenant.

Romans 8:16 does not say, "The Spirit bears witness that you are outperforming your peers."

It says we are children of God.

That identity doesn't fluctuate.

It doesn't compete.

It doesn't panic.

When you understand that, comparison loses its power.

And a rubber band loosens.

CHAPTER 5

Discouragement is a Decision

Discouragement often feels inevitable.

It feels justified.

Logical.

But discouragement becomes dangerous when it becomes agreement.

Sitting in that parking lot, I was facing two thoughts.

Thought one:

Utah had 100 sales.

Idaho had zero.

Thought two:

I was a failure.

Thought one was factual.

Thought two was interpretation.

Discouragement is built on interpretation.

It says:

"This will never turn around."

"You're not capable."

"You should quit."

But none of those statements are facts.

They're predictions fueled by fear.

Elijah once called down fire from heaven.

He saw miracles.

Then one threat from Jezebel sent him running into the wilderness, where he asked God to take his life.

One threat erased a mountain of miracles in his mind.

God didn't shame him for that.

But He didn't confirm the discouragement either.

He strengthened him.

Fed him.

And sent him back.

Discouragement is real.

But it is not sovereign.

It only gains authority when you agree with it.

Galatians 6:9 ends with four critical words:

"If we faint not."

Not fainting is a decision.

You may not control outcomes.

But you do control surrender.

You control whether you move forward one more step.

When I chose to knock on that door with toys in the yard, I wasn't guaranteed a sale.

I was simply choosing obedience over emotion, and the sale followed the decision.

Many blessings in life follow decisions, not feelings.

If I had turned back and driven home that afternoon, I would have felt relief.

But I also would have built a rubber band ball of regret.

Discouragement says, "Stop."

Faith says, "Knock on one more door."

CHAPTER 6

THE EXECUTIVE WHO NEARLY BROKE ME

IF COMPARISON AND DISCOURAGEMENT tighten rubber bands quietly, humiliation and injustice tighten them fast.

By this point in my career, I had moved my family across states.

We had purchased a home in Michigan.

I was working seven days a week.

This was no longer a job.

It was an identity.

Then came a company event in Florida.

Meetings during the day.

Recognition.

A cruise afterward.

My wife came with me. I was proud to bring her. She had endured every early morning and late night beside me, and she deserved it.

One morning, I was told that the senior executive over our zone wanted to meet for breakfast.

We walked into the restaurant.

He was already seated.

I introduced my wife.

He didn't acknowledge her.

Not rudely.

Just . . . not at all.

He immediately began questioning me.

"What are your plans for the new promotion?"

"How will you increase production?"

"What's your strategy for next quarter?"

I hadn't even received the full materials yet!

That was supposed to be the purpose of the conference.

With every question, I felt smaller.

My wife sat quietly beside me.

She didn't react.

She didn't correct him.

She simply supported me by her presence.

But inside, something tightened.

I wasn't angry yet.

I was exposed.

Like Adam and Eve realizing they were naked.

And pride does not like exposure.

The Branch Visit

A short time later, that executive visited my branch.

He was a large man. Former football coach. Carried authority like it was physical.

He went out with several of my managers.

When one of my female managers returned to the office, she was upset. She said he had made an inappropriate, dismissive physical gesture toward her.

Something shifted in me immediately.

Up until then, I had absorbed his tone.

But this crossed a line.

I walked into his office and said calmly but firmly

"If you ever treat one of my managers like that again, we will have a serious problem."

He looked at me and said without hesitation

"You will never be promoted as long as I'm over you. You can't run a branch."

It was immediate.

Final.

No discussion.

In one sentence, years of effort felt threatened.

I drove home in silence.

Told my wife what happened.

She didn't panic.

She listened.

But inside me, something darker began to grow.

Anger.

The Journal

That night, I couldn't sleep.

I replayed the breakfast.

The branch confrontation.

The threat.

Over and over.

At first, the rumination felt justified.

Then it became poisonous.

I began wishing consequences on him.

Not aloud.

But internally.

That is where rubber bands form.

Mosiah 3:19 teaches:

"The natural man is an enemy to God . . . unless he yields to the enticings of the Holy Spirit."

I wasn't yielding.

I was rehearsing.

Someone once told me that when you carry emotional garbage, you should write it out.

So I did.

I opened my computer and began typing everything I felt.

Every injustice.

Every insult.

Every reason he should not lead anyone.

Page after page.

Night after night.

At first, it felt powerful.

Like I was building a case.

But I noticed something.

The more I wrote, the more agitated I became.

Doctrine and Covenants 121:37 says,

"When we undertake to . . . gratify our pride . . . behold, the heavens withdraw themselves."

Heaven felt distant.

Not because I was wrong to address inappropriate behavior.

But because I was feeding anger.

The Delete Moment

One night, after typing another page, I leaned back in my chair.

Quiet.

A thought came—not loud, not dramatic.

"You cannot carry this. Give it to Me."

I stared at the screen.

All my arguments.

All my justification.

All my carefully constructed paragraphs.

If I deleted them, it would feel like surrender.

Like losing.

Like letting him win.

But Alma 7:11–12 came to mind:

"He shall go forth, suffering pains and afflictions . . . that he may know according to the flesh how to succor his people."

Not just sins.

Pains.

Humiliation.

Threats.

Injustice.

Christ had already paid for this.

Why was I insisting on carrying it?

My hand hovered over the keyboard.

Then I pressed Delete.

The screen went blank.

And something inside me went quiet.

Peace didn't explode.

It settled.

Within a short time, that zone manager was gone.

A new leader came in and asked, "Why aren't you running this branch?"

And I was promoted.

But that wasn't the real promotion.

The real promotion happened the night I deleted the file.

If I had kept that anger, it would have shaped every decision afterward.

Forgiveness didn't excuse him.

It freed me.

The Return to the Garden

After Adam and Eve sewed fig leaves together, they hid.

But the scripture says:

"Unto Adam also and to his wife did the Lord God make coats of skins, and clothed them" (Genesis 3:21).

He replaced their covering with His.

That is the Atonement.

Until now, this book has shown how the rubber band ball forms:

Comparison.

Discouragement.

Pride.

Anger.

Self-protection.

None of these begins as rebellion.

They begin to hide the rubber band ball.

Now we move to the only thing that unwinds the ball.

Surrender.

CHAPTER 7

The Rubber Band Ball is Born

Years later, I was called to serve as a bishop over a ward of young single adults.

If you've never sat across from a nineteen-year-old carrying shame, you may not understand how heavy silence can feel.

They would sit in the chair across from my desk.

Eyes lowered.

Hands folded tightly.

Voice hesitant.

Sometimes they came because of something recent.

Sometimes because something old had resurfaced.

Sometimes they didn't even know why they felt heavy—they just knew they did.

We would talk.

We would pray.

I would testify of the Savior.

And often, they would leave lighter.

But something began to trouble me.

A few months later, many returned.

Different issue.

Same heaviness.

It wasn't just one rubber band.

It was a ball.

So one afternoon, I built one.

I gathered every rubber band I could find.

Different colors.

Different sizes.

Some thick and tight.

Some stretched thin and fragile.

Some cracked but still tangled into the mass.

Layer after layer, it grew.

By the time I finished, it was the size of a volleyball.

It was awkward.

Heavy.

Unattractive.

And when people handled it, it collected dirt and grease from their hands.

I placed it on my desk.

The next time a young adult came into my office, I picked it up and set it in their lap.

"This," I said gently, "is what you're carrying."

Not just what happened last week.

Everything.

Every memory you never processed.

Every mistake you never released.

Every offense you never forgave.

Every moment you said, "I'll deal with this later."

It was visual.

Concrete.

Real.

And when they held it, something clicked.

CHAPTER 8

The Process

The first instruction was always the same.

Go home.

List every rubber band.

If it still stings, list it.

If it still brings emotion, list it.

If it still shapes how you react, list it.

Some involved a few rubber bands at once.

Some were caused by themselves; some were caused by others.

Some went back to childhood.

Then we worked through them one at a time.

They wrote:

What happened.

How it happened.

How they felt.

What they believed afterward.

Because if it still lived inside them, it was still theirs.

Then came five declarations.

Not symbolic—

literal.

I give this to the Savior.

I forgive myself.

I forgive the offender.

I let this go.

I won't pick this up again.

Then they would take a red pen.

And they would write those declarations across the page until the words underneath were soaked in red.

Those **red-soaked pages** represented the **Savior's blood.**

Tears would fall.

Paper would wrinkle.

It was never neat.

It was surrender.

Doctrine and Covenants 64:10 teaches:

"I, the Lord, will forgive whom I will forgive, but of you it is required to forgive all men."

Forgiveness is not emotional agreement.

It's a spiritual transfer.

It's moving ownership from your hands into Christ's.

Some sessions were quiet.

Some were intense.

Some required multiple visits for one single rubber band.

But slowly, the ball grew smaller.

CHAPTER 9

One Hundred Thirty-Six Rubber Bands

One evening, a young woman walked into my office.

Black hair.

Large, dark glasses.

Black dress.

Black shoes.

It wasn't fashion.

It was armor.

I felt the hurt, pain, and sorrow she was carrying.

I talked briefly.

She stood up suddenly and left without saying a word.

A week later, she returned.

This time, I placed the rubber band ball in her lap.

hoping she would stay a little longer.

As I explained the process of the rubber band ball, tears slid silently down her cheeks.

Then she stood, put the ball on the desk, and left again without saying a word.

Another week passed.

She entered quietly and placed a spiral notebook on my desk.

"I have an appointment at five," she said softly. "I'll be back."

Then she walked out.

I was shocked. I didn't know she could talk.

I opened the notebook.

One hundred thirty-six items.

One hundred thirty-six rubber bands

Some were only a few words.

Some were longer.

She experienced her first rubber band at age eight.

I wept as I read.

These were not minor disappointments.

These were wounds.

Betrayals.

Shame.

Manipulation.

Regret.

When she returned at five, we began.

One rubber band at a time.

Some sessions were filled with silence.

Some were filled with tears.

Some required her to pause for long minutes before she could answer.

We didn't rush.

We didn't skip.

We didn't minimize.

We surrendered.

One by one, the list shrank.

Until we reached number 136.

Her former boyfriend.

She froze.

"I can't," she said.

"I hate him. When you say his name, I feel sick. He made me do things I never should have done. I can't forgive him."

There was no exaggeration in her voice.

Only exhaustion.

Only pain.

She was going home for the holidays and would be gone all of December.

I told her to write him a letter.

Tell him everything he did and how it made her feel.

Then decide whether to send it or burn it.

January

When she walked back into my office in January, I didn't recognize her.

Blonde hair.

Light blue dress.

No dark glasses.

Her posture was different.

Her countenance was different.

She placed the notebook on my desk.

When I saw the tattered notebook, I finally recognized her.

"I'll be back at five," she said.

I opened it.

One hundred thirty-five items crossed out.

The final page filled.

This time, as I read, there were tears of joy.

We met at five.

She told me she had written the letter.

Every memory.

Every wound.

Every betrayal.

Then she wrote about the Savior.

She wrote about how He had already taken 135 rubber bands.

She wrote about how His Atonement was real.

She chose to forgive.

Not because it was fair.

but because she refused to carry him any longer.

As she finished writing, she felt as though the Savior wrapped His arms around her.

She wept.

Tears were tears of joy.

Tears of PEACE.

Then the phone rang.

It was her ex-boyfriend.

He had gone to his bishop.

He had been instructed to ask her forgiveness before moving forward in his life.

He apologized.

She forgave him.

Fully.

Freely.

Back in my office, she wrote the five declarations in red.

The ink bled through the page.

Her tears fell again.

But these were not tears of shame.

They were tears of release.

I stood, embraced her, and said:

"I testify that all 136 rubber bands are gone.

You are walking out of here clean."

And she did.

Alma 7:11–12 became real in that room.

He truly takes upon Himself our pains, afflictions, and temptations of every kind.

Not symbolically.

Literally.

A Testimony of Freedom

A young single adult that I counseled with expressed their experience in the following way.

To whoever may be reading this:

I've sat in that chair.

I know what it feels like to stare at the floor because looking up feels too vulnerable.

I know what it feels like to say "I'm fine" when you're anything but fine.

When Bishop first called me into his office and asked

how I was doing, I told him everything was okay.

It wasn't.

But by the promptings of our Heavenly Father, he already knew it wasn't.

When he explained the rubber band ball exercise, I didn't want to break down.

But I couldn't stop the tears.

I had been carrying something for years.

It happened long ago.

I had promised myself I would take it to my grave and never tell anyone.

I believed that with enough time, it would fade.

That it would stop hurting.

But no matter how deeply I buried it, it kept resurfacing.

I thought there was nothing more I could do.

I thought I would just have to live with it.

If you're feeling that way right now, please hear me clearly:

You do not have to live with it forever.

The process is difficult.

It was for me.

I told the bishop I couldn't do it.

It was too painful to relive.

These were memories I had buried so deeply that digging them up felt unbearable.

But I'm here to testify that it was worth it.

Time has passed since I sat in that chair.

From the moment I completed the process until now, I can say without hesitation that I would not have the peace in my life today if I had not surrendered those rubber bands.

I can now drive to places I once avoided.

I can speak about my past without breaking down in tears.

I can share my experience in hopes that it helps someone else find courage.

When I finished writing and covering those pages in red ink, I felt something lift from me.

Not just emotionally.

Spiritually.

I had always believed in the Atonement of Jesus Christ.

But until you experience His power personally—the release, the peace, the cleansing—you cannot fully comprehend it.

Today, I have an unshakable testimony of my Savior, Jesus Christ.

I am closer to Him than I have ever been in my life.

If I had known how my life would change and how I would feel now, I would have done this much sooner.

Please do not keep holding on to what is hurting you.

There is a reason you are sitting in that office.

Your bishop—and more importantly, your Heavenly Father—wants to take away your burden.

This is why Jesus Christ suffered.

So that you would not have to carry it alone.

I testify that as you surrender it, you will feel closer to your Father in Heaven than ever before.

In the name of Jesus Christ, amen.

CHAPTER 10

Why Forgiveness Frees the Forgiver

Forgiveness is often misunderstood.

It is not declaring someone innocent.

It is not pretending something didn't happen.

It is not minimizing pain.

Forgiveness is transferring ownership of justice.

When Christ suffered in Gethsemane and on the cross, He satisfied the demands of justice.

When we refuse to forgive, we attempt to collect a debt that has already been paid.

And that poisons the collector.

Doctrine and Covenants 64:10 says:

"I, the Lord, will forgive whom I will forgive, but of you it is required to forgive all men."

Notice the structure.

God reserves the right to judge.

We are required to release.

When that young woman forgave her ex-boyfriend, she did not excuse his behavior.

She released herself from carrying him.

That is surrender.

Unforgiveness feels powerful at first.

It feels like control.

But it binds you to the offender.

It ties your emotional life to their memory.

It replays scenes.

It reopens wounds.

It tightens rubber bands.

Forgiveness cuts the tie.

It doesn't erase memory.

But it removes ownership.

Alma 7:11–12 promises that Christ took upon Himself not only sins but pains.

Pains are not always the result of our choices.

Sometimes they're the result of someone else's.

He took those too.

And if He carried them, why are we insisting on holding them?

Forgiveness isn't weakness.

It's an agreement with the Atonement.

What's Next?

At this point, some people ask:
"Now what?"
The ball is gone.
The pages are covered.
The tears have been shed.
What does life look like afterward?
That is where we go next.

CHAPTER 11

You Are Not the Ball

One of the first changes I notice after someone completes the rubber band process is subtle but profound.

They begin to separate themselves from what they carry.

Many people confuse identity with experience.

"I am the mistake."

"I am the failure."

"I am the one who was betrayed."

"I am the one who fell short."

But surrender creates separation.

You begin to understand:

I am not what happened to me.

I am not my worst moment.

I am not even my greatest success.

I am a child of God."

Romans 8:16 declares:

"The Spirit itself beareth witness with our spirit, that we are the children of God."

That identity doesn't rise and fall with performance.

It doesn't fluctuate with approval.

It's covenant-based.

Performance-based identity builds rubber bands.

Covenant-based identity builds stability.

When you truly accept that you are a son or daughter of God, you stop measuring your worth against yesterday's failures.

You stop proving. And you start walking.

CHAPTER 12

Pressure Still Comes

Let me be clear.

Surrender does not eliminate pressure.

Bills still come.

Deadlines still come.

Criticism still comes.

Sin and failure still come.

But something inside changes.

Before surrender, pressure feels personal.

After surrender, pressure becomes a question:

"Is this mine to carry?"

That one question prevents new rubber bands.

Some burdens are assignments.

Some are not.

Christ said:

"My yoke is easy, and my burden is light" (Matthew 11:30).

Notice He did not say there would be no burden.
He said His burden is light.
That means shared.
When you try to carry it alone, the weight increases.
When you yoke with Him, the weight distributes.
Pressure may remain, but strain decreases.
That is the difference.

CHAPTER 13

Leading Without Carrying Everyone

One of the greatest temptations in leadership—whether as a parent, bishop, manager, or friend—is absorbing someone else's spiritual life.

You counsel.

You care.

You love.

And if you are not careful, you begin to carry.

But you are not the Savior.

You are a witness.

Doctrine and Covenants 121 teaches that power flows through persuasion, gentleness, meekness, and love unfeigned.

Not force.

Not control.

Not emotional absorption.

When leaders attempt to carry what Christ already paid for, they build their own rubber band ball.

You can testify.

You can guide.

You can invite.

But surrender must be personal.

When you understand that, leadership becomes steadier.

Less frantic.

Less anxious.

More trusting.

CHAPTER 14

Don't Pick It Back Up

After surrender, something important happens.

Peace settles.

But then, weeks or months later, a memory resurfaces.

A location.

A name.

A familiar feeling.

Many panic.

"I guess it didn't work."

But that's not true.

Memory is not ownership.

Revelation 12:10 calls Satan *"the accuser."*

If a thought produces shame and distance from God, it's an accusation.

The Spirit corrects.

The adversary condemns.

When a surrendered memory returns, don't relive it.

Don't renegotiate it. And don't re-feel it.

Just say calmly:

"That has already been given to Christ."

In 2 Corinthians 10:5, we're taught to bring every thought into captivity.

That includes old ones.

Don't argue with accusation.

Dismiss it.

The Savior doesn't return burdens.

Only we do.

And you don't have to.

CHAPTER 15

Becoming Steady

Spiritual maturity isn't loud.

It's steady.

Less reactive.

Less defensive.

Less easily offended.

Storms still come.

But you no longer build balls from them.

You respond instead of react.

You forgive faster.

You surrender quicker.

You sleep more deeply.

Isaiah 40:31 promises that *"they that wait upon the Lord shall renew their strength."*

Renewed strength doesn't come from proving.

It comes from trusting.

When you stop sewing fig leaves and allow the Savior to clothe you instead, something remarkable happens.

You become steady.

Not because life is easier.

But because you are lighter.

EPILOGUE

You Don't Have to Carry It

I have lived long enough to know something with certainty.

Most of what we carry are things we were never asked to carry.

The Savior is not waiting to condemn you.

He is waiting to lift you.

I testify that the Atonement of Jesus Christ is real.

I have seen shame dissolve.

I have seen anger release.

I have seen countenances change.

He can take what was done to you.

He can take what you did.

He can take what you regret.

He can take what you replay at night.

But He will not force it from your hands.

You must give it.

Fully.

Honestly.

Completely.

When you do, something shifts.

You walk steadier.

You lead more calmly.

You forgive more quickly.

You stop covering, and you allow Him to clothe you instead.

That is my testimony.

And here is my invitation:

If you are carrying something, don't wait.

Write it.

Give it.

Forgive.

Let it go.

Freedom is possible.

In the name of Jesus Christ, amen.

APPENDIX A

The Rubber Band Ball Process

A Step-by-Step Guide to Surrender

1. **Write Every Rubber Band**

   If it still stings, write it.

   If it still triggers emotion, write it.

   If it still shapes your reactions, write it.

2. **Work One at a Time**

   Don't rush.

   Detail matters.

   If it still lives inside you, it's still yours.

3. **Declare the Five Surrenders**
    - I give this to the Savior.
    - I forgive myself.
    - I forgive the offender.
    - I let this go.
    - I won't pick this up again.

4. **Write It in Red**

    Cover the page.

    Let it be messy.

    Let it be sacred.

5. **Walk Forward Clean**

    Don't revisit it.

    Don't rehearse it.

    It's no longer yours.

APPENDIX B

Weekly Rubber Band Check-In

Once a week, ask yourself:

- Did I internalize something that isn't mine?
- Did I rehearse a grievance?
- Did I forgive quickly?
- Did I surrender quickly?

Small rubber bands are easier to release than large ones.

APPENDIX C

For Bishops, Leaders, and Parents

You are not the Savior. You are a witness.

Your role is not to absorb someone's burden. It's to testify and forgive when they surrender it.

Doctrine and Covenants 121 reminds us that power flows only through righteousness, persuasion, and love unfeigned.

Don't build your own ball by carrying what Christ already paid for.

CONTINUE THE JOURNEY

Visit Our Website

Thank you for taking this journey.

If this message has touched your life, your next step is waiting for you.

Visit **therubberbandball.com** to go deeper into the process you've just experienced. There, you will find:

- A closer look at the Rubber Band Ball process
- Opportunities to meet the author
- Information on booking speaking engagements for firesides, youth groups, and meetings
- Free resources to help you apply these principles in your own life
- Testimonials and real-life stories from individuals who have walked this path—share *your* story!

You will also discover how to:

- Obtain a signed copy of the book
- Donate copies to prison libraries, shelters, and homes for those in need
- Share this message by ordering copies for your friends and family

This is more than a book—it's a movement of healing, growth, and transformation.

Your story isn't over.

Your purpose is still unfolding.

And one small step forward can change everything.

Keep going.

– Ron Howard

www.ingramcontent.com/pod-product-compliance
Ingram Content Group UK Ltd.
Pitfield, Milton Keynes, MK11 3LW, UK
UKHW062254290726
14090UKWH00017B/693

9 798894 541297